1973

S0-BOM-425

3 0301 00027316 5

This book may be kept

FOURTEEN DAYS

A fine will be charged for each day the book is kept overtime.

GAYLORD 142			PRINTED IN U.S.A.

AMERICAN CHILD

Other books by Paul Engle

WORN EARTH

AMERICAN SONG

CORN

WEST OF MIDNIGHT

ALWAYS THE LAND

AMERICAN CHILD

THE WORD OF LOVE

AMERICAN CHILD

Sonnets for My Daughters

With Thirty-six New Poems

PAUL ENGLE

THE DIAL PRESS
New York

LIBRARY
College of St. Francis
JOLIET, ILL.

Copyright 1945, 1956, by Paul Engle

Copyright 1945, 1955, by the Curtis Publishing Company

Library of Congress Catalog Card Number: 56-9509

PRINTED IN THE UNITED STATES OF AMERICA

BY THE HADDON CRAFTSMEN, SCRANTON, PENNA.

811.5
E581

For Margaret Stoddard

The second time this book for you—
All the old and all the new—
Because you understood the wild
Wonder of the human child,
Because you found no joy above
Mortal child from mortal love,
Because for all these years you knew
How life and child and sonnets grew.

63610

ACKNOWLEDGMENTS

The author wishes to thank Mary and Sara Engle, who lived this book, and Kitty Fisk, who helped.

Acknowledgment is also made to the following magazines in whose pages certain of these poems have appeared.

LADIES' HOME JOURNAL

POETRY MAGAZINE

ROCKY MOUNTAIN REVIEW

SATURDAY REVIEW

GOOD HOUSEKEEPING

THE NEW YORKER

THE KENYON REVIEW

AMERICAN CHILD

Lucky the living child born in a land
Bordered by rivers of enormous flow:
Missouri talking through its throat of sand,
Mississippi wide with ice and snow,
A country confident that day or night,
Planting, ploughing or at evening rest,
It has a trust like childhood, free of fright,
Having such powers to hold it east and west.

Water edged with willow gray or green
Edges the hours and meadows where she plays.
Where the black earth and the bright time are piled
She lives between those rivers as between
Her birth and death, and is in these bold days
A water-watched and river-radiant child.

Lucky the living child born in a land
Giving each child her personality,
Where she need not believe at a command
Some frantic fable of supremacy,
Where girls dress as they want to every day
No matter what the weather, wet or warm,
Not all alike in an official way,
Mock soldiers muffled in a uniform.

She does not hear each day the radio
Rehearse its formal ritual of rage
Against all enemies, east, north and south.
Her mind, at day's end, moves with her small age,
While fountain-like the cries of children flow
Out of the evening's deep and marble mouth.

View from the Empire State was far-off smoke,
Factories fuming at the scalded air,
Wall after wall until your vision broke
On buildings glaring at the sun's gold glare.
Place of dramatic distance, of ships falling
Down a dark river falling down a land,
A far world with not even one child calling:
Dull to a girl whose world was—touched-by-hand.

But then a boy runs by, and then another
(Males they are, so each one tries to beat),
A squawling brat being shaken by his mother.
She leans toward them with all her loving form.
Her face turns crowded as a city street.
She makes that stone tower feminine and warm.

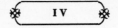

Now she becomes a world
Of words: the furious *I*,
The us like an arm curled
Over her shoulder, cry
Of the demanding me,
The angry yell of you,
The loving word for we,
The questioning of who?

For saying makes things real:
Ouch! is the cause of pain,
Wet is the taste of rain,
Cut is the noun for knife,
Pig is the pride of squeal,
Child is the look of life.

The image of this child would be that willow
Rooted in water, the red bark in air,
And when she falls asleep, her proper pillow
Would be that creek-bank. Green would be her hair.
For she moves lightly as a living bough
Blowing windward on a leaf-light foot,
Yet when she stands still, in the instant now,
Grows downward into earth like a deep root.

For she becomes each natural thing she touches:
Patting a horse, her stern hoof paws the ground.
She turns as stolid as a stone she clutches.
One dusk she climbed that willow, and we found
When the wind merged them, that we could not see
If tree became a child, or child a tree.

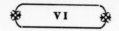

She is a country with its own frontier
Moving each day a little farther west,
Green meadows dotted with the shyest deer,
Great valleys that the raving wolves infest,
Mojave deserts that have such a glare
Each grain of sand flames back one separate glow,
Sierra ranges where the rock is bare
Or buried under ravenous, fanged snow.

As we move through that country, it moves on
Always a range beyond us. If we catch her
Over the last horizon—Swish!—she's gone.
Yet she is more to love by that dear token.
Always she climbs, just as we try to snatch her,
The cliff of childhood, where our hands are broken.

Siren city, with a blonde on every block,
Down the far streets the scream of cops or fire,
All day on the bruised ear the brutal shock
Of traffic on stone buildings yelling, Higher!
She trots along, her eyes just at knee level,
Ignores the people, watches a stray dog,
Moves through that mass, a miniature she-devil
Rising to haunt them from her country fog.

Through all she walks as down a village street,
Then finds beneath a pale tree set in stone
A caterpillar crawling at her feet.
Blind to the windows with their glittering goods,
She picks it up and says, It's all alone,
We ought to take it home to some real woods.

A beach of flesh above a beach of sand.
Tide-steady jaws tearing at food gone gritty
With shattered, golden granite of the land:
The sea-desiring people of the city.
She dives around them like a dolphin leaping
Over and under the fish-furious waves,
Past buried bellies and the sunburned sleeping,
Past papers where the world's old madness raves.

Like something dragged by the delirious tide
She flings up to us out of breath and streaming
Glittering water down from neck and side.
She says, I'm tired, falls off to sleep, her head
Curled on my arm, smiles from her beach of dreaming
Narrow along the world's wide sea of dread.

She hears the voice say, Estimates go higher
On millions dead from H-bombs. No defense.
Then, as the curious wood says, What is fire?
She asks, But what is *that*? And her intense
Voice trembles as she adds, A bomb? The thought
Shakes her like a dog an old felt hat.
She lifts her head in trust and anguish, caught
Between her love of us, and fear of *that*.

Under the golden fall-out of the stars,
Enduring our knowledge like a dread disease,
We wait in silence. Then the whole room jars
As she screams, I'll ask *her*, and with a wild
Crying hugs her doll, while my arms seize
The live, exploding element of child.

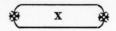

Sliding one day, and laughing, over the snow,
Their sleds collided, and the angry boy
Held up his bleeding fingers, yelling, Oh!
And swore at her until the living joy
Bled to death across her frantic face.
But took his hand, I'm sorry my sled tore it.
Don't worry. Let's go over to my place.
I'll fix you up. I'll get a band-aid for it.

She got a bandage, wrapped his hand with care.
He watched her fingers in their rapid motion,
And said, You're nice. I didn't mean to swear.
She touched his face and smiled, Now, that job's done.
Her sudden incandescence of devotion
Brightened his face, made warm the winter sun.

Home she wore like a defiant harness
Until she ran away, then ran back scared,
Her only hope, to fall away from farness.
Nothing mattered but the life we shared.
Before, adults and fools, we thought she must
Live wholly alone in her pure childlikeness.
But then she grabbed our hand and clung. Her trust
And need fell on us like a loved caress.

Once, we thought, with all her private cares,
She wandered, lost, in a wood of childhood, wild
With trees of terrors, where adults were bears.
That night we learned from her, in shame, intense
Wisdom of human closeness, from a child
On whom we forced our own false innocence.

1.

I punished her for an
Act she did not commit,
Punished her, like a man,
Because she would not admit.
Then learned—and evil came
Powerful in that place.
It had a face and name.
It had my name and face.

But through her blinding, white
Tears of innocence
She said, Oh, that's alright.
I shook, who had defiled
A life, at such offense
Forgiven by a child.

2.

I knew that my defeat
As foolish-proud adult
Was inner and complete,
But as a last insult
And with defiant guile,
Lifting my shameful eyes,
I let the bold lips smile,
Feeling so wicked-wise.

Silence. The shriek of time.
And then I saw above
Her bare girl-agony
A smile of wonder climb,
As she gave back to me
Her woman-wise, old love.

FIFTEEN

Partly a man's, partly a river's, daughter,
She dives from the bank, and does not need to beg,
And drinks with all her body the cool water,
Letting its current flow through arm and leg,
Swimming above, below, the surface, slick
As trout, until she tires and comes to land,
On the wet sand-bar draws a girl with a stick,
Drawing her doom on the dissolving sand.

She is a double image, girl and fish,
Home in two elements, so twice as knowing,
Daft with duplicity, she has learned how
To make her life both bony fact, loved wish,
And is two people: Child that splashes now,
The woman toward whom all her life is flowing.

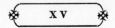

The brakes squealed on the bricks like a stuck hog.
She saw the furry body on the street,
Stroked with her eyes the suffering, loved dog.
There at the window in that August heat
She shivered inconsolable and cold
When, like a cup of milk abruptly spilled
Her fear flowed over her face, and she was old
As human grief, knowing that it was killed.

She had that dog from the moment of its birth,
Taught it to sit and beg, to fetch a ball.
She turns her weight against the turning earth
To slow down bloody time, and beats her head
On the wall: I want it. *My* dog isn't dead.
And want it! Want it! Want it! Screamed the wall.

Her eyes, like some deep-mined, heart-colored stone,
Draw in plain daylight and bleed out pure brightness.
Inside her shoes, each miniature, live bone
Leaps like birds in all their feathery lightness.
She runs in from her playing and we know
There is a skin beneath that backyard grime.
She sees the dirt, but only laughs to show
The child beneath the now beneath the time.

Once at a grown-up party in she walked
In perfect form, like a parade with banners,
Smiled, showed off her newest tooth, and talked.
But then turned stubborn and refused to move,
Waggled her ears, put out her tongue, to prove
The child beneath blue dress beneath good manners.

She held the slimy worm, but couldn't bear it,
Dropped it in disgust and muttered, Ish!
If that's what crawls around a healthy carrot
I'll never eat another one. I wish
Dirt wasn't dirty, and that bugs were birds,
That good clean air was all a cabbage needs.
Walking as she spoke, she dropped her words
Down the long garden rows like growing seeds.

That night she came in hungry from her play.
Dirt was on her like another skin.
What can I eat? she questioned. I'm all in.
Dabbles her hands in water, starts to fix
Her hair, when suddenly we hear her say,
Oh boy! My favorite supper. Carrot sticks!

As dogs will run in their dog-desperate worry
That they'll be left home from the picnic park
And hurtle down the stairway in a furry
Hysteria of paw and tail and bark,
She wildly jumps with her girl-harried hurry
From stair to landing, in a pink-dress arc,
And screams out in her voice's frantic flurry:
Don't go, don't go, don't go, it's getting dark.

From that gray corner where she had been shoved
By fear that we would go as the sun was going
She runs to us as if she fled a far
Dangerous country, laughs in shrillness, knowing
We hold her tight. The glow of being-loved
Rises in her like an evening star.

We look at the map. She asks about the names
Of all the rivers, islands, capes and bays
Called by familiar George, Anne, Charles and James,
Neighborhood kids, it seems, with whom she plays.
I tell her they were royal and great
Who ruled huge kingdoms from a crimson throne,
And made their life in history a date,
Had children who played far too much alone.

She listens seriously, and then says, Anne
I sort of like, and Charles is, well, O. K.,
George is a dope and tries to be a man,
But Jimmie, I wish he'd come out and play.
I don't want any place named after me.
I only want to be right here, and *be*.

She asks: May I go too? And lifts her small
Face, with nothing in it to insist
But hope like a familiar animal,
Begging to be picked up and teased and kissed.
In doubt, in wanting, in anticipation,
A smile flies from her mouth like a tamed bird.
Her slightest gesture is an accusation
That I will not say—Yes!—the simple word.

Before my—No!—I let the pure emotion
Of love beat on me like bareheaded rain,
Enduring her child-desperate devotion.
She will go anywhere, however far.
If she saw Jacob's Ladder, she's so vain,
She would beat the Angel up it, stone to star.

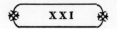

One day she fell down hard and broke her arm,
Climbing the tree to keep up with a boy.
He laughed when she fell screaming, not to harm,
But in a human, horrible, scared joy
That he was safe. In bed, in pain, that night
The white wall howled, gray floor howled back, she
    found
A glare of yell in the electric light.
Blackness beyond the window was loud sound.

One day he called. She laughed right in his ear.
He left in rage. She laughed and said, So long.
But later, healed, playing beneath that tall
Tree without him, she looked up to hear
High in those brutal branches the gay song
Of sparrows waiting for a god to fall.

She packs two six-guns, wears a western belt
With horns and cattle brands to hold blue jeans,
Her rocking horse leaps up as if it felt
Spurs on her bucking broncho boots. She leans
Forward, and suddenly that dull room changes
As she yells, Yippee! the old cowboy cry,
Becomes the wild west myth, tremendous ranges
Where free men ride forever, under free sky.

Dusty with all that distance, she dismounts,
Dropping her reins, and makes her horsy joke:
Breakin' the tough ones in, the rider counts,
He's got to have good hands and a thick hide.
She pats her wooden horse and says, He's broke.
He's safe, now, for anyone to ride.

XXIII

When she came back in fear
Because she lost her dime,
The whole world fell like a tear
On the troubled cheek of time.
She weeps as for some deed
Too terrible to name.
Out of her eyes tears bleed.
Her body shivers shame.

Foolish and yet right:
Emotion ought to be,
However great or slight,
Of such intensity
It gives to sunlight, light,
And teaches teeth to bite.

63610

LIBRARY
College of St. Francis
JOLIET, ILL.

With the child standing there, we read the news
Aloud, the furious episodes of fate,
A flooded town, liner lost on a cruise,
But most of all we marvel at the hate
Of all those distant countries, screaming at
You and me, the child, with such brute blame
For the world's wrongs, that even children spat
The word, American, like a foul name.

Am I American? she asks. We say
Yes. She begs, Can't those kids come for fun?
I don't hate them. They can use my toys all day.
We plead, Remember, always, men have perished
So you might say, I don't hate anyone.
Cherish a land, where the free child is cherished.

Words were like dogs, to handle, teach and hold,
Live things all colors, gray or brown or gold,
That could sit up, say what you wished to say,
Or bark in stubbornness and run away.
Sometimes she cornered one and it would growl
And give one violent and human vowel,
Or she would chase it through the yapping air
Then sit down bawling in her black despair.

One day she tried to tell about her fall
When a boy tripped her on the hard school ground.
She caught no words in her shocked indignation,
Strangled and stopped, but then in child-elation
Of bitterness, she turned and told us all
With eloquence of face, without a sound.

Yearning to ride that rocking horse alone
He knocked her down, and hooted in disdain.
She learned hate as one learns about a stone,
By touch, by roughness, by sharp edge of pain,
And learned that under what is live and human
A great ape swings across the branching blood.
Wholly, humbly, miniature a woman,
She learned man came from the ecstatic mud.

So turned away and trudged all morning through,
Wearing her grief out as you wear a shoe,
By walking, walking on the wandering earth.
But later loved him, proving there is no worth
Better than what a foolish boy can find
In a girl's instinctive need for being kind.

Standing at the stair top, poised, alone,
With one long breath she seems to fall away,
Begins her morning like a boy-thrown stone,
Plunging through the deep pond of her day.
Ravaged by rest, she runs from room to room,
Turns the dull light bulb to a rage of sun,
Drives daylight in, as if her only doom
Was to get earth turning and her life begun.

We tell her, Dentist today. Her daring flight
Collapses, all the world turns into teeth
Snapping at her, furious to bite.
She falls backward into abysmal night.
Fear shivers in her, as a stone beneath
A moving water, seems to shake in light.

I'm home! I'm home! I'm home!
Runs in and bangs the door,
Throws down her books and comb,
Coat, mittens, on the floor.
Waits doubtfully, then calls
Again, fearing her fear,
When the room's empty walls
Cry, No one! No one here!

Then turns and runs outside,
Finding us waiting there,
And says in her small pride,
Clutching my hand with care,
And dropping one dark tear,
I'm here! I'm here! I'm here!

So far she flees from us, as if admitted
To the shy world of chipmunk, rabbit, fox,
As if the hill came toward her and submitted,
Wavering grass and badger-burrowed rocks,
To her small feet. Now she is all horizon,
Distance-delighting as a scared quail's wing,
Fluttering feather which the warm wind lies on:
No running child, but just a natural thing.

Leaping away, she turns to wave defiance
But stumbles, and her head cracks on a stone.
Silence. A cry. Then her proud self-reliance
Falls broken to the ground in its wild dearness.
Her life one scream, Don't leave me here alone,
And all her love a total need for nearness.

Sewing her awkward stitches on the bed
She stuck her thumb, yelled, Damn! to her own
   surprise.
She bit the word off like a chunk of bread
And spat it in our face. Her startled eyes
Looked at us, half in pride she knew the sound,
And half in fear, like a suspicious cat.
We scolded, sent her to her room. Her round
Mouth mimicked us, tongue out, with, I'm a brat.

But shame crept through that house on heavy feet:
A punishment too hard for crime so slight.
We went up to her room, to save her night.
I said, I'm sorry, all the fault was mine.
So tight she clung, I felt the small heart beat
While love grew in her like a watered vine.

Teetering up and down in their child sharing
They both yelled, Faster, in ecstatic sound,
Then he jumped off in some dark boyhood daring,
Battered her head and faith on the frozen ground.
She lay there, silent, in a frantic fog
Of rage and pain he could not understand.
She played with her disaster like a dog
That licked her face, then bit her in the hand.

She ran and told us her tear-scalded story.
Then he came back. In pride she stopped her bawling.
I'm sorry. That was a dumb trick, he said.
She smiled in pleasure-pain, nodded her head,
Having learned in one wild flash, appalling
Human nature in its grime and glory.

She sickened. We could tell
That when she closed one eye
Half the blue light fell
From half of the blue sky.
Then sat and watched all night
On her high hills of sleep
The lost and mad and white
Goats of terror leap.

The fever broke and fled,
Ending her blood's dark strife.
Morning came, to lay
Over her troubled head
The healing hand of day.
And we returned to life.

If everything around me is just air
Why can't I fall straight up as well as down?
If yesterday was here, then when is where?
If I'm alone with dolls, then what's a town?
If streets and dogs are numbered, who counts why?
How many pennies jumping in a handful?
If birds are like black screams in the blue sky
How much gold sound is blowing in a handful?

I touch a cat. It jumps. That means it's me.
The air's the world, but what I breathe is mine.
I'm looked at by the solid things I see.
If I speak to my watch and it says nine,
Because the sun climbs up and down all year,
Then where is when, how far from now is here?

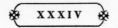

Home from school, she told about the mouse—
Her hands leapt like it in their narrow rage—
White and tame, it scuttled through no house,
But squeaked and circled in a narrow cage.
Dazzled by daylight and her story's fun—
She needed no safe cage or place to hide—
She ran from us, under the bragging sun,
To squeak and circle in her human pride.

That night, excited still, almost a brat,
She said, I can't sleep now, ran out to chase
Strangers and friends and dogs until they fled.
But then the furry dark turned fanged and cat,
She ran into the house, her room, her bed,
And hid in a cage of sheet her crying face.

Don't be a fool, I said.
She turned with such a stricken
Look I hung my head
And felt my belly sicken.
I watched indignant day
Watch her indignant face.
Would any word I say
Regain her shattered grace?

I knew that no loud lie
Or brag would help her live,
Or even let me hide
My piety of pride
That did not let me cry,
I am the fool. Forgive.

Planning her day, what she would do, and where,
She walked upon the lightness of her hope,
Acrobat of joy in the balanced air,
Like a performer on his lively rope.
From room to room she hustled, and caressed
Every toy and doll with every sense.
Only in motion could she ever rest;
Quiet, for her, meant simply to be tense.

Later the boy came by and gave a yell.
She ran to the window. He was just her age.
But he went on to see the girl next door.
Silent she trudged upstairs, and from that floor
We heard all morning, as from a struck bell,
The bronze reverberation of her rage.

We say, now that's a real goose-feather sky,
Wonder what kind of weather it will bring.
She looks up with a startled, bird-bright eye,
Waiting to feel the falling of that wing.
Lost in the wide landscape of looking, she
Still believes the marvelous myth of seeing:
Touched-by-eyes is the one reality.
She gives up to that vision all her being.

For her, mere daylight is ecstatic sight
And nothing visible is really far
When eyes like hands can stroke the violent light.
Plain morning sky is one immediate star.
Through all the apparent world her child-belief
Drifts, as on autumn air, the dazzled leaf.

In another incarnation
Surely she would be,
By climbing exaltation,
A long-tailed lemur, free
To screech his indignation
While hanging from a tree
And dropping perturbation
Down on you and me.

But she is only girl
Glaring from a bough,
With one offended curl
To shake against us now:
Part animal still wild,
Part angel, and all child.

She is a little continent complete
With two blue lakes where every object drowns,
Two proud peninsulas of legs and feet,
A plain of face filled with familiar towns,
Her mouth is a small cave from which birds fly
Over the cleft cliff of her chalk chin,
Along her back are fields of sun-brown rye,
Rivers of heart-rainfall flow through her skin.

And in her head are reckoning and rock,
Mountains of hope whose ranges have no name,
Where days float down like feathers without shock,
Beaches where she may walk without a mark
At night along a foaming shore of shame,
Moving from darkness into utter dark.

She touched the old piano as an old
Man will fumble at a new machine,
Marveling, troubled, and afraid to hold,
Uncertain what each polished part could mean.
She struck the tooth-white keys and made them shout
And jumped in fright while her pale forehead frowned,
She pulled her ear to shake the music out
And looked between her fingers for the sound.

She questioned—Where? Suddenly it was in
Her voice, the round and living vowel, as she
Cried it was gone, not knowing in her thin
Body all taut experience took root
Behind the bone, and grew there like a tree,
Green and many-branched and bearing fruit.

Her day is object, it, the actual fact,
Known from the one sure place where her feet stand,
The simple move, the clean and casual act,
Not the large meaning, motive, will, demand.
She thinks of rivers not as the abstract
Force of flow, but wetness poured on sand,
The flame, the finger where the nerves contract,
Not the idea of pain, but the hurt hand.

She walks through worlds of puzzle, wagon, stone,
The heard and held, the hard and tasted real:
A truer time then nights lying alone
When sound will bring hysteria of fear
And the loosed lightnings of her hands reveal
Nothing around her like an atmosphere.

Her doll was not just lying on the floor
But stretched to hear below-rug creatures talk.
The man shattered it as he swung the door:
Don't throw that stuff where people have to walk.
Each fragment fell in her eyes and made them blind.
Each word dropped on her eardrum like a rock.
Across the savage forest of her mind
Shambled the fanged and growling bear of shock.

Swiftly she lives. Slowly she learns in time
That her small world lives recklessly beneath
A world whose hands and feet make casual crime
And yet are never punished. With intense
Carefulness she lives, and with clamped teeth
Endures her one crime, which is innocence.

The air was soft as her red lung that breathed it,
The sweet sunlight was one huge honey-comb,
Her face was calm as the long wind that wreathed it,
Covering cloud, nest, tree were all her home.
She bent down where a row of iris grew.
Just as she plucked the bloom a church bell clanged.
She screamed, and in that savage instant knew
The noise of flowers was bronze from the loud sky
　　banged.

And in one start of bitter apprehension
It seemed to me her last and gravest walk.
Unmoving there in terror and in tension
She waited for the marvel to occur:
Her face the flower, her leaning hand the stalk,
While earth was reaching up to gather her.

Touch is learned by letting fingers taste
Leaf and dog and doll. She learns to hear
By letting frightened noises in their haste
Crawl into the friendly cave of ear.
She learns the form of rattle, rock and tree,
And even, in her wisdom, knows not-being.
When blackness of her night is blinding she
Learns to use eyes to learn about not-seeing.

She knows the natural earth of thing, but all
The human world is dreadfully ahead.
Yet she will keep the strength of simple land
And like a redwood widen and grow tall,
Her life not merely love, grief, friend, but bread,
Not understand, be understood, but stand.

She lived with animals of her own size:
Wren by her window; once she found a frog
In a bird bath and so with outraged cries
Drove it away; and once she had a dog
And had no rest until the consummation
Of crawling in its house on the foul floor;
And there was a whole day of indignation
When a real fishworm crept beneath her door.

One day she pushed a kitten in the pool
And was astonished when its quick breath bubbled
Two or three times and stopped. That night in cruel
Punishment we watched while in her gloom
The little mouse of her heart ran tame and troubled
Through her remorse and through her tight-walled
room.

The clean day climbing over earth is raised
Above her narrow house like a child's hand
Lifted in love because someone has praised.
I watch her at the eastern window stand,
Her face on fire with morning, darkness under
Her feet, and while her sleep-gray hands grow white
Her empty eyes fill with their daily wonder
At the fantastic fact of light, light, light.

Then she is out of doors, and suddenly
She is herself a small and furious sun
Lifted over the ground where her doll lies.
She moves above the wide fields shiningly,
Loving the living earth where her feet run,
Making that whole land meaningful and wise.

Tall people talked of time—Five minutes more.
Looked at a watch and said—Last hour, next year.
But time was something crawling on the floor
Between the strange foot falling and the fear.
They spoke of space and measured nothingness
With hand or stick or the tense height of a boy,
But she knew space was solid hopelessness
Between the frantic finger and the toy.

Time was terror. But one night she found
By merely waiting, wanting, morning turned
Into a hand comforting and consoling.
And space was that green length of level ground
Where once she threw a yellow ball and learned
That world was in it, round and lost and rolling.

She walks like a grave kitten on a fence
Between two clear realities—below,
The earth where all is heavy, feared and tense,
Above, the air where all is light, cloud, snow.
Dirt is where you hide things when they're new,
Wind is used for flying and for birds.
Day in her eyes is buried under blue.
Her hands are the live fluttering of birds.

Growing old does not mean growing wise
But losing what was accurate and wild,
The savage sense of river, sound and sun.
Deafened by ears and blinded with our eyes,
We will forget the elemental child
Is made of earth, air, water, fire in one.

From what dark sleep and stupor of the stone
The breathing figure of a man arose—
A gasp of air within a bend of bone,
With twisted guts and brain and curling toes—
We do not know, but here in the light it stands
A length of marvelous and talking mud,
While all the generations lift their hands
Stirring the cupped infinity of blood.

From her light sleep and strenuous awaking
Instantly lifted hand and tongue and eye
Move to the paper doll that she is making,
While deep in her and on the mouth that smiled
There runs another spirit with no cry:
Immortal childhood in the mortal child.

L

Already she has known nights when the warm
And sultry air is heavy on her heart
Until her face is slapped with cold, and storm
Tears the hot and solid sky apart.
Lured by lightning in the summer sky
Children half-frightened and all eager under
Threatening dark, run out and wait with dry
Tongue for the dry and noisy taste of thunder.

So she ran out, looked up, and saw a place
Shining beyond the sky beyond her hand.
Yet her eyes brought it right inside her head,
And she learned then, live lightning on her face,
That fear was force you didn't understand,
And terror tasted otherwise than bread.

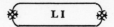

Books were the actual world she touched and knew
Where trolls were real and friendly goblins hid
Under the bed, and gentle dragons blew
Smoke from their mouth and talked the way she did.
Wolves between the covers of a book
Wandered all day their safe, familiar land,
Brown squirrels came down from colored trees and took
Imaginary acorns from her hand.

She became those books. She was the girl
Locked in a high tower in the gray Scotch highland.
She was the fisher's wife with a crown of pearl.
And when they told her of the shipwrecked man
Named Crusoe, she became herself the island,
The beach, the footprint where the stranger ran.

Monkeys were metal with a shining thing
Stuck in their bulging belly, which you wound
Till it was tight and legs began to spring
Up and down with a gay, grinding sound.
Bears were small and smooth with a neat head
That could be washed, and paws that they would keep
Out of their food, and if they went to bed
With you, they were the first to go to sleep.

That childlike wonder in a childlife world
Lived until a living monkey yelled
Horribly from his cage, a brown bear hurled
Filth at her, who suddenly saw that these
Real beasts were more unreal than toys—they smelled,
Were huge, could not be touched, and scratched for
    fleas.

Now she is all the seasons in one child:
Her eyes are summer and the summer sun
Full with a great earth warmth, open and mild,
Her hands are autumn when the crop is done,
Her rapid fingers harvesting ripe touch,
Her hair is winter drifted with blonde snow,
Her mouth is spring and overfilled with such
Cry as you hear when the webbed ducks northward go.

For all her life is the enormous now,
No time is in it, and no yesterday
Torments tomorrow asking why or how.
The intense instant is complete and right.
Forever is a place as far away
As the dark forest or tomorrow night.

She listens valiantly while violins
Worry about the wolf and running boy,
Then grows excited as their music thins
And kettle drums crash out a desperate joy
When duck is safe from wolf and she from fear.
She does not know when music will be all
Her living strength. She in a later year
Will lean upon that wonder like a wall.

A boy, a wolf, a duck, the hunted ground,
Have their small life in her. They imitate
Future intensity when she has found
A skillful way to lift her head and hear
The curved, ecstatic hand of sound create
Enormous countries in the narrow ear.

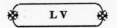

Old people did a wonderful, strange thing
Called dying, though they couldn't tell her why.
There would be flowers and hidden girls would sing.
Strangers called relatives would sit and cry.
Nothing that happened in her house could bring
Such real excitement. Some one old would lie
Limp on a bed, and friends would kneel and cling.
Then it seemed mild and marvelous to die.

They argued with her. She would still believe
Dying did not mean absolute not-being,
But only one loved power you had to leave:
Not to touch rag or ribbon, not to call
A stray dog, maybe terribly not seeing,
Maybe not hearing. One. But never all.

For the first time she felt adult and wise,
With the small power a parent has all day
To order sleep and food, to comfort cries,
To argue strictly over noise and play.
Their games were gay or solemn, in the worst
She had a gun, the kitten was a bear.
Yet when it died one night she knew her first
Real and undeniable despair.

Forgetting the times that she was scratched or bitten
She only recalled her love for a live thing
And first learned grief and loss in one gray kitten.
At the brief burial she was tall and brave,
But as the gray fur fell she had to fling
Her grave child hands over the gravel grave.

In that time when it seemed the simple weight
Of delicate daylight crushed her living eye,
She knew that, night or noon, early or late,
We would be there to hear her smallest cry.
That knowledge of our nearness, strength against strain,
Held firm when fever carried her too far,
And in the falling darkness of her pain
That power rose in her like an evening star.

So we gained faith and health from her grim sickness,
And she grew stronger as she lost her strength,
Refusing, with her whole body, resignation.
And when at last mind, hand won their old quickness,
She held her arm toward us all its thin length,
Lifting her love against annihilation.

Her thin cheeks narrowed by November cold
She ran indoors and cried—It hurts, this place.
Her hands grown suddenly aware and old
Were little bird feet walking on my face.
All of her frozen but her forehead burning
She crept to bed and whispered once—That's nice.
Her eyelids dropped. I felt my whole life turning
Numb as a nerve packed for too long in ice.

All night infection, stealthy, secret, crawled
Around the room, around her forehead's flame,
And by her beating throat crouched grim and clawed.
Morning she called my name in desperation,
Then, in a queer voice, called again my name
With a dark humor that was adoration.

She lay in bed while her limp bones were shaken
By fever furious that so frail a child
Should go on breathing when her breath was taken.
Once, blood burning through her skin, she smiled.
Expert in pain, she watched with powerless eyes
Agony make its narrow, neat incision,
Then the delirium and the blind cries
And death was in her like an indecision.

All night we stood, the way her stuffed bear stands,
Awkward, waiting for a fist to strike.
Space broke apart between our rigid hands.
Morning brought miracle, the pure perfection,
For when her eyelids opened it was like
Rocks rolled back before a resurrection.

Child who cries,
I cut this place,
Child with eyes
Blue as space
Watching the world
Upward climb
Over the curled
Finger of time,

Remember this:
We grow tougher
Only by pain.
To walk, still sane,
By the abyss:
Learn to suffer.

She wore the morning like an affirmation,
Never would hot and hungry noon arrive.
Each little word was like an adoration
Of tree, bird, touch, light, smell that meant—Alive!
No difference in being and not-being:
Her gingham cat was running everywhere,
The button eyes of rag dolls glared with seeing,
Even her doll grew desperate for air.

It was a day when every living thing,
When rook and rock and field all joined in her
To praise, shout Yes, to live in trust, to please.
To talk on that day meant, for her, to sing.
She heightened all. That night she did not stir
In her child sleep, intensity of ease.

LXII

Landscape means places where she had been lost:
Country of crying very far and dark,
The window wilderness gone strange with frost,
The street of fear, long, curved, without a mark,
The day that she was first left all alone
And felt herself fall through the empty house,
The field where she first found a tiny bone,
Without believing it had been a mouse.

She makes a continent inside her mind:
A fever valley where all day she fled,
A meadow where a bee had stung her blind
And pain pursued her with a golden beak,
A mountain where she went to hide her head
And keep her reticence an unclimbed peak.

SIXTY-FOUR

The night is eating me, come quick, she cried.
My feet are gone. Don't let it get my arm.
She pulled the covers up, wanting to hide,
Her tongue a bronze bell clanging out alarm.
Night was a monstrous mouth, open and black,
Crawling the bed, consuming her beneath,
With no sound but her hammering heart, and back
Of night crept total terror with white teeth.

A darker darkness than mere night will take her
In later time, when all her childlike skill
At crying, at self-comfort, will forsake her.
But now, in the sudden courage of our word
She calls, too loud, I'll bite it back, I will.
And looks around to see if night had heard.

The picture was a young man slightly vain
In uniform, gold braid, cap stiff with wire,
But we remembered an old man, proud with pain,
Fumbling the hands of his past before a fire.
Grandfather, soldier, in the end a plain
Citizen troubled by his gut and soul,
In that same bed his mother once had lain
Waiting for death which makes our living whole.

She asks. We try to tell her: There is a part
Of that man in you, with his laugh, his coarse
Cavalry trooper's talk, his red young heart.
But she is baffled, not believing he
In a blue coat, riding a foundered horse,
The beans in his belly cold, was history.

Tearing off her reticence, the way
We peel the tight bark from a live birch tree,
She told us the layered sorrow of that day:
She pushed him down and hit him with her knee,
And would not let him up, not knowing why,
And would not lead him where his hat was thrown,
And laughed when he ran. Then told us with a cry
How shame struck through her like a falling stone.

We could not give the power of pure forgiveness
But only wait and watch humiliation
Enter, and live in her own pure aliveness,
While like a homeless pup who came to whine
Remorse snarled loud at her in accusation
And grief grew on her like a guardian vine.

Always those who pushed beyond the border,
Mad for the mountain none had ever seen,
Found it, but in the end no calm recorder
To write down how, their one last stinking bean
Eaten, their teeth chewing on blind chance,
Around them every night the wild throats growling,
In hunger half torment and half dark trance
They ate the strange white fruit and died howling.

So she went out into the night, and when
The darkness snarled at her she snarled right back
And grimly marched on where she meant to go.
We found her lost, but she was not in flight.
Her pride was on her like a traveller's pack.
There's nothing here, she said, except more night.

She is a miracle like daily light,
As warm, as moving as that luminous air.
Let her eyes never lose the daily sight
Of the sun's great golden hand on face and hair.
Let all her talk be water from a sweet well,
Tasting of sandy earth, the deep drowned stone.
One sudden day, with strangers, we will tell:
Here is a girl. But look—a woman grown.

Let her live, then, so she may understand
That final, negative and human crime:
Not to learn, in the false fear of too much,
The secret and intolerable touch
From passionate mind and intellectual hand
Of love that knows times when it can know no time.

Child, remember the moment of our birth
Is the same instant that begins our dying,
And for as long as we endure the earth
All of our future is a troubled trying
To learn—do we die at midnight, or next day,
Suddenly from infection's sly erosion,
Or will the time-bomb of the heart delay
For three score years and ten its dull explosion?

Yet in that time we do not wholly die.
The memory of us outlasts our breath.
For we are scattered among all who cry
Our name, or knew our hands and face, giving
Year after year, darkening year, our death
An uttered life longer than our living.

In a white dress, on white feet, through a white day
She flew over green grass lightly as a wing.
Tense in her unpremeditated play
She looked no child, but creature, person, thing
Triply in one creation tied, yet still
Warned at the sight of us, grown-up—be wary.
New, she seemed, with an animal tough will
That daylong furious running would not weary.

Morning and noon and afternoon, all play:
Lost on the lawn, under the lilac creeping,
Hunting her life. She would not eat all day.
Under the porch, her secret hiding place,
I found her. When she woke from that dark sleeping
She hid her face in my hands to hide my face.

History, to her, is another land
Where great men did great things, but quite alone,
And then walked out to public parks to stand
Until they turned to marble men of stone:
Men not scared of night, who had not seen
Bushes change to bears, or felt elation
Merely that morning came, friendly and green,
After sleeplessness and desperation.

There were no women in that land, or few,
And not as mother, but as loved by men.
For them no stone with words that they had spoken.
And never girls who wondered how they grew,
Who fed a golden pheasant in his pen,
Or cried all day because a doll was broken.

Nothing can grieve her like another's grief,
Merely to see it is an accusation,
Her hands lift toward you and the willed relief
Creeps along them like a consolation.
For long in her short living she has known
That gesture meaning—Come. Be reconciled.
Look, I am here—Giving it she has grown
More a woman, and so more a child.

For that one moment she is old and sure
And motherlike is ravaged with remorse
Until she chokes in her own miniature
Fists the evil that is all your troubling:
Then calm flows out from her like a live source,
Bare to our sight the clear spring in her bubbling.

Hallowe'en. She dressed up in a sheet,
A paper crown, a tail, a fierce expression,
High-button shoes, not fitting, on her feet,
A broken mask, her proudest child-possession,
A lantern on the handle of a broom,
While over the sky of her anticipation,
Shining and far away though in that room,
Feet, lantern, hands leapt like a constellation.

Outdoors she waved her lantern in wild daring
And yelled at a stranger passing in the night,
Half to cheer herself and half in play.
But scared herself with her own sudden scaring,
And ran from what she thought would run away,
And found she could not even frighten fright.

She knows blue heron, water-wading bird,
Squirrel planting acorns in the sprouting ground,
Rabbit, fugitive, owl-wary, furred,
Cricket chirping careful, liquid sound,
Green grasshopper eating greener weeds,
Tiger kitten with a twitching tail,
White teeth of gray mouse eating golden seeds,
The terrible, tight moving of a snail.

Let her remain in part an animal
Knowing that under her new skin there lies
The ancient pulse beat with its rise and fall.
Let her voice keep that old blood in her cries,
Let the decisions of her days be all
Animal simple, which is human wise.

For her each day begins with a tin horn
That she can blow until her cheeks turn pale;
It calls up frightful figures not yet born
Or a rag bear with bells hung on his tail.
She is a part of that world, though in play,
That lives when tin or golden trumpets speak:
Boy Blue found sleeping on the field of hay,
Or Roland plundered on the bloody peak.

For her all worlds are one world and her tin
Bugle calls creatures that she cannot feel,
That move, feed in her, are her life alone.
Yet she will learn that all world is not in
Her hands, that no man desperate for the real
Can tear his skin off and be pure, bare bone.

For her the sun comes up natural and clear,
As simple light, not source of month and minute;
She takes as wise and proper warmth and year.
This is her world and we live briefly in it.
She holds space in her hands and eyes with ease.
Time is that instant when the night turns real.
Deep in her head are small philosophies
Of want, dislike of don't, and like of feel.

She does not think how other worlds would be.
This way of earth is definite and good.
New day is not a ripe eternity
For her to taste with unbelieving tongue,
But one more chance to walk beyond the wood
And touch the same low grass where birds had sung.

Fish and frog and fear are in that pool
And little snakes that vanish with a lunge,
And eyes that stare up at her from the cool
Water where the hand-dropped pebbles plunge.
Hours she will lie and wonder how they walk
Below, and begs me not to use a hook,
And asks if, when they see her there, they talk
A loved and secret language meaning—Look!

Today she held one hand beneath until
It turned as pale as light, and she forgave
That pond for boats it pulled down silently.
Wise in water, watching it fierce or still,
She will not wander when a deeper wave
Will rise and flood her with eternity.

Evening comes now like a punishment
Because the game-filled day had been too good,
And bed is bitter when magnificent
Lions roar all day in the chair leg wood.
Later, the years when daylight comes like claws
Tearing your face where the dark terror stood,
When day looms like a punishment because
Night, oblivion-blessed, had been too good.

Her days are still delight, play, animation,
When dolls grow hungry too and must be fed
And simple darkness is a desperation.
Yet one small wisdom holds against the night:
She knows one call out of her troubled head
Will bring my hand, more luminous than light.

She answers yell of boy or song of bird,
Calls to the green snake rustling on the ground.
Talking or listening she acts each word.
She is herself all sounds and hears each sound.
But there are times, hearing us call her name,
When she stands rigid, dreading our dislike.
Looking at us in fear that is our shame
She waits for the coiled and cunning tongue to strike.

Wanting in pride only to join her play
We shattered it, forgetting we cannot go
Into her solid world, forgetting we know
That talk can bring us not one word-width nearer,
That even her answering voice is far away
As the echo of a cry made in a mirror.

She knew the night we brought a strange box home
And shrewdly found the place where it was hidden,
And knew it was a gift, and guessed for whom,
And knew that looking for it was forbidden.
Morning she opened it. A doll. And ran
Into her room and closed the door, intending
Secretly to play and make a plan.
But knew at once there was no use pretending.

She came out with a little furious pride
Over her face, thinking how clever, trying
To prove that she had nothing there to hide.
But when we looked at her the live shame spilt
Over her face. She knew. She broke out crying
And shook in her first agony of guilt.

She moves, a human creature marvelous
With rounded rib the lacelike lung enfolding,
Ravening tongue tasting the fabulous
Water and food of earth, with hand for holding.
Head on its nimble neck, turning and lean,
Is lifted with its eyes of furious fire
Above her body like a Hallowe'en
Pumpkin raised on a stick to make it higher.

And in that head the intolerable mind
Already tattered with the hunt for—Why?—
Whose rage is all the certainty she'll find
Although the cold sweat crawl on her hand's palm.
Yet in that fear she will not cease to try
And in that conflict will be all her calm.

Each morning she looks up and breathes the sky
And marvels again that night and day are varied.
Breathing, she does not wonder at what cry
Of woman, crow, or bell that wind has carried.
Each day is an astonishment of breath
She warms by the nourished blood, yet unaware
That all the dark astonishment of death
Is merely the lung emptied of mere air.

She breathes that insubstantial element
That turns to substance: body, nerve and pain.
Yet there are days of absolute content
When all her laughter is a hollow house
Raised against sorrow and the raving rain
While she lives in it like a patient mouse.

Look, she called, I'm learning how to build.
In her excitement she began to stammer,
Holding her work up, proving to us how skilled
She had become with nails and wood and hammer.
It was an awkward box just one doll deep.
I saw her in a box, all out of breath,
Who made, before that dressed and doll-like sleep,
Hardly enough living to make a death.

So once in sandy Palestine there crawled
Over the floor of his father's shop a little
Boy with dull knife and long brown hands, who hauled
Scraps for his own inventing. He would toss
The new work up to show how he could whittle:
Look. I'm learning. I can make a cross!

Watching her watch the hover of that hawk
I think that birds should fly out of her eyes.
Watching her hear the wren on that corn stalk
I think her speaking should be all bird cries.
When autumn haze floats up as a rain-warning
She turns as insubstantial as the fog,
When warmth and light move through a summer
  morning
She strokes the day as if it were a dog.

For she becomes herself the handled thing,
All that she feels, the looked-at crystal, night.
Affection turns her something wholly wild.
Lift her and watch, for holding up will bring
The color in the crystal in the light,
The loving in the living in the child.

Where is north? Is there a north in me
Where I'm the only person that can go?
I think there is, and in it I can be
Cold when I want to. I can make it snow.
She thought of that and shivered. Where's the real
North in the world? Maybe I can take
My own north there, and maybe I can feel
How cold a snow two norths together make.

And she will go on asking for direction—
The naked north, the evening west, bird south—
Until, so gently there seems no connection
Tomorrows fall on her like drifted snow
And she drives back that question in her mouth,
Knowing that she knows she will never know.

Nothing in heaven but the arrogant sun,

Nothing in earth but the green lust for growing,

Nothing in water but the nervous flowing.

At night we practice winding in a sheet

And death whines—Good. You'll like it once you try it.

But fresh day comes at last and we can eat

Time like bread. Yet we are eaten by it.

No certainty but our old worn awareness

Of brown or blue eyes staring at white swans.

And then she comes with her frail certain fairness,

Figure of calm and fury reconciled,

With eyes of burning agate, bones of bronze,

In calm magnificence of child as child.

Good-bye is the grim word. She knows already
It is the sound for sorrow that will come
In month and year, to lean on her its steady
Weight. But still the nerve will not grow numb.
So when he left she had only a headful
Of that word pounding in it like a hammer,
While all the day with that one word was dreadful
And sleepy night pronounced it with a stammer.

He went away in storm. But still on clear
Days the rainfall of that memory clattered
Inside her mind, and lightning lunged so near
She knew (and could not spell) it meant one word.
And in between her hands the thunder battered
One sound—Good-bye! Good-bye! Until she heard.

The sky was just another earth for those
Grown old and tired, we told her. There were all
The fields with cows and crickets, trees with crows,
Gardens where the fat white grubs would crawl.
Look, she cried, I'll pick some pears for you,
Lifting her arm in the quickness of her joy,
Where stars were fruit—grape, apple, plum—and grew
Beyond a wall that would baffle only a boy.

She turned in slow grief toward us and her face
Was sanded with one long desert of despair.
Her hands fell as if separate in space.
In shock, in awkward shame, and in disgust,
We watched our lying legend grip and tear
Her marvelous mythology of trust.

She struck it without asking right or wrong
To see if it was sleeping or awake,
But jumped when from its hissing mouth the long
And looking tongue ran like another snake.
The mottled skin she knew and did not fear,
But that live tongue was terror, for it came
Secretly from the body, inward, queer,
And burned her morning calmness like a flame.

Familiar pain shocks less than strange delight.
For her the fanged and furious dog next door
Frightened less than the soft touch at night
Of furred, fantastic, nameless shapes that stood
Silent until she woke and saw on the floor
Her real fear running the imagined wood.

Her dog, tongue out, tail friendly, seemed to float
Over the field. But a man rushed out with a great
Cry and kicked him in the ribs and throat
For nothing but the ecstacy of hate.
She suffered every blow in every bone
And did not want to see, but would not leave,
And learned of foulness she had never known,
And learned of evil, but would not believe.

Yet when she knelt and her indignant hand
Fell with incalculable grief and lightness
She learned all evil lived where all men stand,
Snarled from the earth and the breathed air above,
And knew then in a sudden blinding brightness
That love is hate of all you do not love.

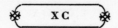
Who cares for stars in their multitude of sky?
Her round and open eyes can hold them all.
What matter if clouds seem great gulls as they fly?
Her hands have their own graceful rise and fall.
Infinity is limitless, pure space?
She runs from room to room in her pure play.
Eternity is time beyond time and place?
She lives from game to game and day to day.

Her breath defies the emptiness of air.
By subtle body is she called a daughter.
All of her meaning is: Alive. Now. There.
Her whole life is a crystal, for the light
Cuts through it and the colors flow like water
And all that flow is blood, is living-bright.

Look, she called, the mirror's in my face,
Then laughed to find her face was in the mirror,
And learned the power of each thing in its place,
And all the worlds in her one world came clearer:
A world called see for looking at the sun,
Another world for touch and one for hear,
A world for taste and one for smell, and one
Large and dark and everywhere, for fear.

All of those worlds are in her, and they grow
Cell by secreted cell and bone by bone
To merge in one long memory named—know.
And then the years when world is merely—be.
No past, no future, an old woman alone
Remembering the time when she had memory.

XCII

Triumphant child whose thought is instant act,
The mind fluttering in her finger tips,
Never the word retained until abstract
But once imagined, leaps from the waiting lips.
So when she fell and snow like a cold blaze
Crawled down her back, it told her what to feel:
She laughed in her logic, knowing there are days
When laughing is the one action that is real.

When the boy next door gave her his favorite truck
(Only one wheel was lost) she could not praise,
But for that long astonishment of luck,
Holding the truck toward us in fierce appeal,
She wept in her wisdom, knowing there are days
When tears are the one action that is real.

The sound went in her ears and out her eyes,
Even her mouth helped, making the word for watch.
The ticking troubled like an insect's cries.
She heard the wheels turn, each in its neat notch.
She laughed and questioned—When can I have one?
Time was tick, not loss or a forgetting.
She saw no kinship between watch and sun.
Night was merely moonrise and moonsetting.

But time will come when she will learn that time
Is the one human term of final worth,
When she will watch all night the cold death climb
Up a child's throat, and slowly understand,
And twist her arms around the turning earth
And slow it down by scream and tearing hand.

The boy next door owned toys she had never found,
And best of all a marvelous blue boat
With wheels that rolled it over grass and ground,
Yet in a pool of water it would float.
All other toys moved in one element,
Truck on the land, kite on a length of string,
But the blue boat was doubly different,
Less like a plaything than a living thing.

One evening she left it on the walk
And it was smashed, her first enormous crime.
He wept accusingly, unreconciled,
Until she touched him without any talk,
With one warm hand, and was for the first time
In act a woman, though in hand a child.

The boy next door came over with his bear
(Made of brown cloth and mounted on four wheels).
She got her favorite doll (it had one ear
Missing, but danced by springs hid in its heels).
Their play went on, half silly and half solemn,
She took from him, he gave to her, delight,
And in that room their talk climbed like a column
Of smoke from a house where all was warm and right.

Then each gave each the loved toy, and with such
Ease, as if they knew in this one motion
That love, which is at first the bitter will
To live by taking, each from each, word, touch,
Grows in its fulness to the better will
To give, by each to each, depth, calm, devotion.

She looked with glad and grave eyes at the boy
And looked in her own self in her blue vision,
And half held out and half held back the toy
In her extremity of indecision.
So all the motives of her mind revolved
Around her gray dilemma—how to live—
And head and hand were taut as they resolved
That moral anguish—keep for myself, or give.

But suddenly she turned and let him take it
With speed that was to both of them surprise,
And watched him play, and trembled as if naked
In such an agony of exaltation
That living tears were torn out of her eyes
And her whole body was an incantation.

The boy next door came over. Innocent
She gave him all the toys on all the floors,
And through the little house of her excitement
Ran, opening windows, banging doors,
So lost in ecstasy that her hand shook.
Gratitude and gift were all her mind.
But when she stooped to get her favorite book
For him, he laughed and struck her from behind.

The savagery of the scared mouse is monstrous.
So in the fury of her fear she turned
With one mad shout, almost delirious,
Beating him with her book until it split,
And learned revenge in violence, and learned
All that revengeful shame that follows it.

Lucky the living child born in a land
Where mouth and mind and morning all are free,
Where any man lifts up his open hand
In no salute but simple liberty,
Where, when they frighten children, it is still
With beasts imagination can create,
Monsters of fire that live beneath the hill,
And not the dark, blood-reckless, dreaded state.

"They are listening. Look out." That wild
Warning we have not heard deep in our bone,
When not one child could trust one other child,
When not one girl confided in another.
She, in America, has never known
The monstrous child whisper against her mother.

Lucky the living child born in a land
Where noise outside the door is still a dog
And not the secret gun, the bloody hand,
Where fear is not around her like a fog
Dark and cold and desperate for her throat,
Where books are still merely the children's choice
And not self-glory that a leader wrote
With an hysteria of hands and voice.

No child need learn a mouth has many ways
Of talking, lies, deceit, intimidation,
Still in this day her cries for games she plays
Are not the slogans of a state oration,
But the old calls of children in all days,
The living triumph of the tongue's elation.

C

Lucky the living child born in a land
Whose fault and lack are publicly admitted,
Where men affirm the ground on which they stand
Without fear that their lives have been committed,
Where men dare state their difference with the state
And walk out in the daylight unafraid,
No child is fed with artificial hate
Nor puffed with flags, mass marching and parade.

Let this, her land, be always such a place
Where having freedom is like having bread,
Where the clean landscape of a new child's face
Is seldom by the boast of blood defiled,
Where on its streets and alleys without dread
Plays all day long the proud spontaneous child.

This new and expanded edition of an already highly praised and much beloved volume of one hundred sonnets contains thirty-six poems that have never before appeared in book form. A sequence of one hundred sonnets is a rare event. What makes AMERICAN CHILD even rarer is that Mr. Engle has invented many variations of the traditional form, finding a flexibility in new shapes and rimes in order to express the widest range of childhood experience. The new verses—numbers three through thirty-nine—were written while Mr. Engle traveled across America and were inspired by his younger daughter, Sara—by the "new things she and her friends were doing and saying." The previous poems were written for Mr. Engle's older daughter, Mary, some ten years ago. Taken together, the sonnets form a picture of how it is to be a child in America today. As Mr. Engle writes: "I am trying to define the never-returning uniqueness of childhood, that sudden awareness of the world which the adult can never have again. I also want to show the good